# Festivals *of the* World

# INDIA

Gareth Stevens Publishing
**MILWAUKEE**

Written by
**FALAQ KAGDA**

Edited by
**ELIZABETH BERG**

Designed by
**HASNAH MOHD ESA**

First published in North America in 1997 by
**Gareth Stevens Publishing**
1555 North RiverCenter Drive, Suite 201
Milwaukee, Wisconsin 53212 USA

For a free color catalog describing Gareth
Stevens' list of high-quality books and multimedia
programs, call
1-800-542-2595 (USA)
or 1-800-461-9120 (Canada).
Gareth Stevens Publishing's Fax: (414) 225-0377.
See our catalog, too, on the World Wide Web:
http://gsinc.com

Printed in Singapore

© TIMES EDITIONS PTE LTD 1997
Originated and designed by
Times Books International
an imprint of Times Editions Pte Ltd
Times Centre, 1 New Industrial Road
Singapore 536196

Library of Congress Cataloging-in-Publication Data:
Kagda, Falaq.
India / Falaq Kagda.
p.   cm. — (Festivals of the world)
Includes bibliographical references and index.
ISBN 0-8368-1683-8 (lib. bdg.)
1. Festivals—India—Juvenile literature.  2. India—
Religious life and customs—Juvenile literature.  3.
India—Social life and customs—Juvenile literature.
I. Title.  II. Series.
GT4876.A2K25  1997
394.2'6954—dc20          96-27330

1 2 3 4 5 6 7 8 9 99 98 97

# CONTENTS

# It's Festival Time . . .

Whatever your religion, whoever you are, there are plenty of festivals for you in India. Whether you're Muslim or Sikh or Christian, farmer or merchant, there's a festival specially for you. And with every festival, there's a *mela* [MAY-la] that goes with it (that means "fair" in **Hindi**). Come along, take a ride on the Ferris wheel, go on an elephant ride (or do you prefer camels?), and buy some pretty jewelry. Put on your best clothes because it's festival time in India . . .

# WHERE'S INDIA?

India takes up most of southern Asia. It is a huge country and more crowded than almost anywhere else in the world. One person in every six people on Earth lives in India. The country has everything from the highest mountain range in the world on its northern border to hot tropical jungles in the south. At the heart of India are the Indus and Ganges rivers, which bring life to the plains around them. The Ganges is sacred to Indians. The capital is New Delhi. India also has other very large and crowded cities, such as Calcutta and Bombay.

## Who are the Indians?

There are many different kinds of people in India. Those in the South are smaller and darker than those in the North, and there are many variations in between. Long ago, **Caucasians** moved from Persia into India, where the dark-skinned **Dravidians** were already living. Over the centuries, they have mixed and created people of many different colors and features. Indians speak a variety of languages and have widely different customs. Most Indians are Hindus, but there are also many Muslims, Sikhs, Christians, Buddhists, and Jains.

A smiling Indian girl wears a garland of flowers, ready to go to a festival.

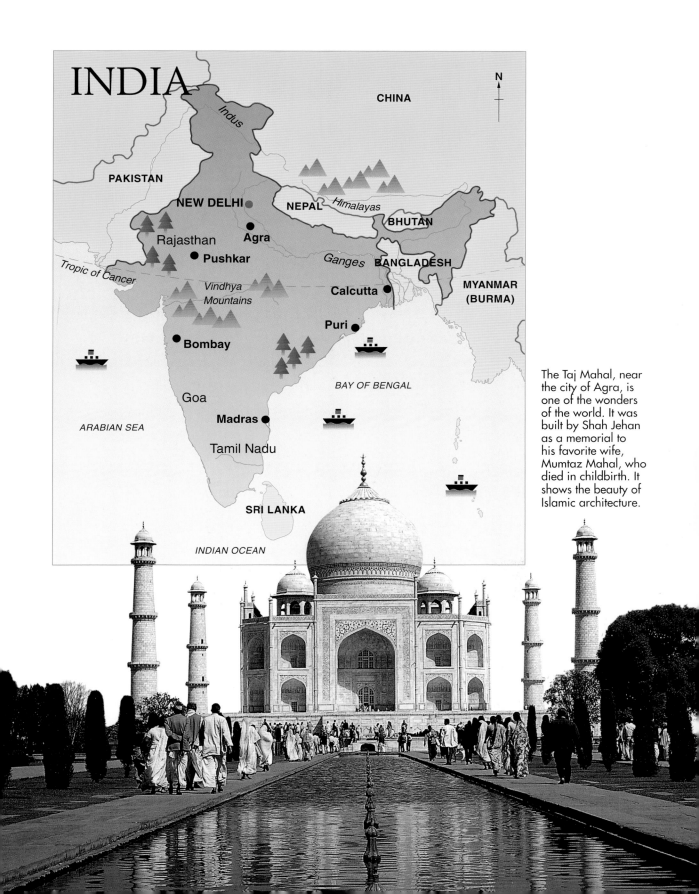

# INDIA

CHINA

N

*Indus*

PAKISTAN

NEW DELHI

NEPAL

*Himalayas*

BHUTAN

Rajasthan

Agra

Pushkar

*Ganges*

BANGLADESH

Tropic of Cancer

*Vindhya Mountains*

Calcutta

MYANMAR (BURMA)

Puri

Bombay

Goa

BAY OF BENGAL

Madras

ARABIAN SEA

Tamil Nadu

SRI LANKA

INDIAN OCEAN

The Taj Mahal, near the city of Agra, is one of the wonders of the world. It was built by Shah Jehan as a memorial to his favorite wife, Mumtaz Mahal, who died in childbirth. It shows the beauty of Islamic architecture.

# WHEN'S THE MELA?

Indians use three different calendars. Hindu festivals follow a special **lunar** calendar. This calendar follows the phases of the moon. The dates of these festivals change from year to year on the Gregorian calendar (that's the one you're probably used to). Muslims follow a different lunar calendar. Their festivals move back 11 days every year, so they aren't even in the same season from year to year.

## SPRING

- **BASANT**—For this celebration of spring, people wear something yellow. Often there are kite-flying competitions.
- **MAHAVIR JAYANTI**—Celebrates the birthday of Vardhamana Mahavira, who started the Jain religion. Jains come from all over to visit their shrine at Gimar. ✪ **HOLI** ✪ **POORAM**
- **BAISAKHI**—Sikhs celebrate the New Year at this time. They have a big meal together at the temple, then dance the *bhangra* in the streets in the evening (look at page 11 to see the bhangra).

*Want some color in your life? Join me for Holi on page 16.*

## SUMMER

- **RATHA JATRA** (The Chariot Festival)—Images of Krishna and his family are dragged through the streets of Puri on huge chariots. It takes 4,000 people to pull one of these chariots.
- **INDEPENDENCE DAY**
- **RAKSHA BANDHAN**
- **NAAG PANCHAMI**

*Come monkey around with the animals on page 20.*

# AUTUMN

- ✪ **DUSSEHRA**—The festival of the mother goddess, Durga. Statues of Durga are carried to the Ganges River and thrown in.
- ✪ **DIVALI** ✪ **PUSHKAR MELA**
- ✪ **GANDHI JAYANTI**—Celebrates Gandhi's birthday (October 2).

*The Republic Day celebration starts on page 8.*

# WINTER

- ✪ **GURU NANAK JAYANTI**—Sikhs celebrate the birthday of Guru Nanak, who started Sikhism. ✪ **REPUBLIC DAY** ✪ **PONGGAL**
- ✪ **CARNIVAL**—Christians in Goa celebrate Carnival with a traditional red-and-black dance, where they wear all red and black.

# MUSLIM HOLIDAYS

- ✪ **MUHARRAM**—The anniversary of the day the Prophet Muhammad left for Medina, which marks the beginning of the Islamic religion. There are processions in honor of Husain, the Prophet's grandson, who was killed on this day.
- ✪ **ID-UL-FITRI**—Marks the end of the fasting month of Ramadhan. People wear new clothes and have big feasts.
- ✪ **ID-UL-ZUHA**—People kill a sheep to eat in memory of Abraham's willingness to sacrifice his son Isaac.

7

# REPUBLIC DAY

Have you ever seen a National Day parade with elephants painted up in bright colors? If you haven't, come to New Delhi on January 26th for Republic Day! While elephants and camels march down the street, airplanes put on an air show. There are people in all kinds of dress from the different regions of India. Dancers show off the dances of their region. What a show it is to see all these peoples come together to celebrate their country!

## Come to the parade

On a low hill in the center of New Delhi is a red sandstone palace where the president of India lives. Below is a grassy mall. This is where the Republic Day parade takes place. Long rows of wooden bleachers are set up. In the center is an armchair under a gold umbrella. The president sits there to review the parade. Troops of horsemen ride past wearing red coats and gold turbans. Next come the elephants, their trunks painted with flowers. Soldiers and sailors, boy scouts and girl scouts, and patriotic groups march past in their uniforms. Then come the floats representing the states of the Republic of India. Each is brightly decorated to show off the best of its state.

This elephant is decorated to march in the parade. National heroes have the honor of riding on the elephants.

# What is Republic Day?

Indians have two independence days. Republic Day is the anniversary of the day in 1926 when Indians declared their independence from Great Britain. India also celebrates Independence Day, the day 20 years later when the British turned over power to Pandit Jawaharlal Nehru, India's first prime minister. On Independence Day, the president makes a speech. But the real show takes place on Republic Day, when the weather is cool and it is a nice time to sit outside and watch a parade.

A corps of women soldiers marches in perfect form.

The camel corps from the desert region of Bikaner is one of the high points of the parade.

# Independence

Many years ago, India was a colony of Great Britain, but Indians wanted to run their own country. They thought the British were using India to make themselves rich, while Indians stayed very poor. People believed they had to force the British to leave. But the British were strong, and the Indians had no army. What could they do?

## A great man

Mohandas K. Gandhi was a leader of the Indian struggle for independence. People call him Mahatma Gandhi. *Mahatma* means "Great Soul." He believed that it was wrong to kill anyone. He thought the best way to make the British leave was to refuse to obey unfair laws. He called this "passive resistance."

## Make your own salt

When the British put a tax on salt that made it very expensive for Indians, Gandhi announced he was going to make salt himself. He started walking to the sea, which was 150 miles (240 km) away. As he walked, people joined him. Finally there were thousands of people marching. When people saw this, they realized that the British couldn't tax them without their consent. After many demonstrations like this one, the British were forced to leave.

When he was young, Gandhi wore pants and shirts, but later he wanted to be closer to the common people of India, so he started to dress like a simple farmer. He also learned how to spin yarn and wore hand-woven clothes. People loved him because he shared the life of the simple people.

Dancers come from all parts of the country to represent their local area. Here, a troupe of Sikhs dance the **bhangra** in the parade. Sikh men never cut their hair and cover it with a turban as a mark of their religion. Guru Nanak started the Sikh religion to bring Hindus and Muslims together. He wanted to show people that God was neither Hindu nor Muslim, but included both.

### Think about this
India has been independent for a short time, but it is a very old culture. Indian ideas and Indian stories have changed many countries. In the United States, Martin Luther King, Jr. borrowed Gandhi's idea of passive resistance and used it in the Civil Rights Movement.

# Let's dance

After Republic Day comes a two-day festival of music and dance. India has its own forms of music and dance that go back thousands of years and are admired all over the world. *Baharat Nhatyam* and *Kathak* are two types of traditional dance. Kathak dancers wear bands with rows of bells on their ankles. They make a rhythm with the bells as they move.

India is famous for its beautiful **sitar** music. The sitar is a large stringed instrument that makes a sound very different from any other instrument. Ravi Shankar is a famous sitar player. With the sitar you are likely to hear the **tabla**, a kind of Indian drum. Zakir Hussain is a popular tabla player.

Indian dance was at first a way of worshiping the gods. Most dances tell a story about gods or heroes.

# DIVALI

I t's late autumn in India, and the long nights are dark as the moon comes to the end of its monthly cycle. On the last days of Ashwin (that's the Hindu month that falls in October or November), rows of small, flickering clay lamps appear in doorways, on windowsills, even lighting the outlines of towering government buildings. These are the lights of Divali [dee-WAL-ly], the Festival of Lights. Divali is dedicated to Lakshmi, the Hindu goddess of wealth and beauty. During the five days of Divali, Lakshmi visits houses and shops that are clean and well lit. And with her she brings wealth and good fortune, so all of India is lit up to invite her in.

## A new beginning

To get ready for Divali, Indians buy new clothes and clean and maybe paint the house. Shopkeepers start a new year, and everyone pays off what they owe. Divali is a time to start fresh, with the hope that Lakshmi will bring better fortune in the next year. Hindus go to their temples to honor the gods. Then they come home and eat special meals. Later they visit family and friends, bringing gifts of sweets. It is traditional to give sweets at Divali. Want to know how Divali started? Listen to a story . . .

A Hindu goddess is decorated for Divali. Hindu gods and goddesses often have several sets of arms to show how powerful they are.

# The Demon of Filth

Once there was a demon named Naraka. Naraka was very dirty, so he was called the Demon of Filth. He never took a bath or cleaned his house. He kidnapped young girls and took them to live in his dirty house. One of those girls was Lakshmi.

Krishna (one of the most popular Hindu gods) fought with Naraka and won. As Naraka was dying, he felt sorry that he had made people unhappy. He asked Krishna to make the anniversary of his death a day when people would be happy. That day is Divali. People celebrate by taking scented baths and dressing up in new clothes.

Here are rows and rows of sweets, flowers, and fruit laid out as offerings to the gods.

Divali lights on a street in Rajasthan.

# The lights of goodness

*Divali* means "row of lights." On the long, dark nights of Divali, the lamps remind people that goodness and wisdom are stronger than the forces of darkness. There are many stories that people tell about Divali, but all of them are about the triumph of good over evil. Here's another story about the victory of good over evil that is part of the Divali tradition.

Lights invite Lakshmi to bring good fortune. A tradition for young girls is to set Divali lamps afloat in the river. If the light burns as long as its owner can see it, she will have good luck in the next year.

One of the stories that goes with Divali is that of the hero Rama's return to his kingdom. Here people use dance to tell the story of Rama's adventures. These dance dramas are popular throughout Dussehra and Divali.

# Rama comes home

Many Indian festivals celebrate several things at once. Divali lights also remind Hindus of the story of Rama's return to his kingdom. According to the story, Rama, an Indian hero, was unfairly sent away from his kingdom. Then the demon Ravenna kidnapped Rama's wife. Rama spent 14 years searching for her. Finally there was a big battle, and Rama destroyed Ravenna. When Rama returned to his kingdom, the people lit lamps to guide him back.

During the holiday of Dussehra [duh-SHEH-rah], which comes just before Divali, people put up giant statues of Ravenna. At the end of the festival, they put firecrackers inside the statues and set them on fire. Divali is when Rama returned to his kingdom. On that night, Indians light lamps to celebrate Rama's return.

Here are statues of the evil Ravenna and his son and brother ready to be set on fire.

15

# HOLI

If you're in India one day in March and someone comes up and throws red powder all over you, don't be surprised. This is Holi, and on Holi people walk around yelling, "Holi hai, Holi hai" and throwing colored water or powder at anyone they see, even if it's their teacher or the mayor of their town. During Holi, everyone is equal and everything is forgiven. The important things are "rang, ras, and rag" (color, dance, and song). So get in on the fun, throw a little powder, and join in the dancing and singing. This is the Festival of Colors. All the rules are off.

Some people use bicycle pumps to squirt red, yellow, and green liquid over everyone.

## A fun time

On the first night, the young men and boys make a huge bonfire. People have to watch closely around Holi or their fence might end up in the bonfire. Men and boys dance around the fire, sometimes jumping through it. Food that has just been harvested is put on the fire as an offering. The next morning, the fun begins. Besides the color throwing, there are huge fairs and circuses. People forget whatever fights they have had with anyone. It's a time to start fresh.

Powders of different colors are offered for sale on the streets. These colors usually wash out of clothes without too much trouble. But I wouldn't wear my best dress on Holi if I were you!

# Beating up the boys

Near Delhi, the women of one village pretend to have a fight with the men of a nearby village. The women carry long bamboo poles. They try to hit the men with their poles. The men carry leather shields. They dodge through the crowds, trying to escape the women. When the women get tired, the men shout insults to get them started again. It's all in fun, and everyone has a good laugh.

Although Holi is a Hindu festival, it is a big carnival that people of all religions join in. A nice thing about Holi is the way it breaks down barriers.

In the evening, people change into clean clothes. They get together in public squares to eat, drink, talk, and watch local folk dances.

# The Holi story

There are many stories about Holi in different parts of the country. The best known is about a young prince named Prahlad. Prahlad worshipped the god Vishnu. He was very religious. His father wanted everyone to worship him. He was very angry that his son refused to obey him. He asked his evil daughter, Holika, to help him punish his son. Holika had the power to walk through fire without being burned. She carried Prahlad into a bonfire. People heard terrible screams and thought that Prahlad was burning to death. Finally, Prahlad walked out alone. His faith had protected him, while the evil Holika burned. That's why there are bonfires for Holi today.

**Think about this**

Does your family do a spring cleaning? At one time, trash was taken out and burned in bonfires during spring festivals. This was a way of getting rid of the remains of winter and starting fresh. In the United States, people still have a day of practical jokes once a year—do you know when it is? (Hint: It's close to the same time as Holi.)

*Opposite:* People also remember the god Krishna at Holi. This is a painting of Krishna as a cowherd. When he was a boy, he was very mischievous and was always playing pranks. He stole milk from the milkmaids. To get back at him, they threw colored powder on him. That is why people throw colors at each other during Holi.

# Celebrating springtime

Holi is also very much like many other spring festivals around the world. Many people celebrate the return of spring with bonfires and a noisy festival where people act wild and crazy. It is a time to be happy that winter is over and food is starting to grow again. In India, the spring wheat harvest comes around this time of year.

# FOR THE BEASTS

Animals have an important place in Indian life, and Indians have a great respect for them. There are several festivals in India that are for the animals, to thank them for their help during the year. For Pooram, elephants wear gold head ornaments in a parade. The men riding on the elephants carry brightly colored umbrellas and peacock feather whisks. Naag Panchami is the Festival of the Snakes. People give milk and flowers to snakes that live in the temples. A special event for camels is the Pushkar Mela.

## Come to the fair

Melas, or village fairs, accompany many religious festivals in India. There are also special melas where people come to trade animals. People come to the fair from all around, dressed in their best clothes. Stalls sell everything you can imagine, from pots and pans to jewelry for the women, fruits and vegetables, and cows and horses (or camels!). There are magic shows, street dances, puppet shows, and circuses. No matter what their religion, everyone enjoys a mela!

A Rajasthani couple take a ride around the fair on their camel. People from Rajasthan wear traditional clothes different from those in other parts of India. Women often wear nose rings, like this woman.

# The camels visit Pushkar

Once a year, the little town of Pushkar in Rajasthan (find it on the map on page 5) comes alive with the biggest camel fair anywhere. People come from the deserts around Pushkar to trade camels and enjoy the fair. There are camel races and camel beauty contests and singing and dancing. Merchants sell everything a camel needs, like colorful saddles and embroidered cloth covers with little mirrors. In the evening, thousands of campfires light up the desert night, and the sounds of folk melodies fill the air.

A camel shows off the tricks it is able to do.

On the night of the full moon, people take a dip in Pushkar Lake. The lake is sacred to Hindus.

# Ponggal

Hindus believe cows are very special animals, so they don't kill them. In Tamil Nadu, a province in southern India, they have a festival where they honor the cows. It's called Ponggal, which is also the name of a sweet treat made from rice, milk, and brown sugar. Part of the Ponggal Festival is to make ponggal treats and offer them to the gods. Ponggal celebrates the rice harvest, so they use the new rice they have just picked. After they offer it to the gods, everyone shares the treats. They also offer the gods clay statues of horses to thank them for sending rain for the growing rice.

Women take advantage of the holiday to look around the marketplace. They have their hair decorated with flower garlands for the festival.

**Think about this**

Many Indians are **vegetarian**, especially in southern India. That means they don't eat any meat or fish. Jains are entirely vegetarian because they believe it is wrong to hurt any living creature. Many Hindus are also vegetarian.

For Ponggal, people like to decorate their front steps. They take powdered chalk or colored rice flour and paint designs on the tiles. These are called **Rangoli designs**.

# Thanks to the cows

On the third day of Ponggal, it's time to thank the cows. The men and boys take the cows out and give them a good bath. Then they paint their horns. Blue and gold are favorite colors. They hang garlands of flowers around their necks and put bright feathers in their hair. Often there are parades and music for the cows. They get to eat some of the ponggal, too.

# Let's play tag

At the end of the day, people have bullfights. But they don't kill the bull like people do in some other countries. In India, they put a packet of money between the horns of the bull and garlands of money around its neck. Then men try to snatch the money away. Sometimes it can be dangerous for the men.

A cow is dressed in its festival best for Ponggal.

# RAKSHA BANDHAN

There is no Mother's Day in India, or Father's Day, but there is a day for brothers and sisters. It is called Raksha Bandhan. On this day, sisters tie a bracelet called a *rakhi* [RAH-kee] around their brothers' wrist. The rakhi is supposed to protect the brother from anything bad that might happen in the next year. The sister also puts a dot of red powder on her brother's forehead and gives him treats. In return, the brother promises to care for his sister and gives her a present.

## Special friends

Even after they've grown up, women give rakhi to their brothers and make them treats. In return, a man might give his sister a new sari. It is a way of saying that even if they fight sometimes, they will always care for each other. Sometimes women "adopt" a brother for Raksha Bandhan. This could be a friend they feel especially close to. They then become "Rakhi brother" and "Rakhi sister."

A group of men show off the rakhi their sisters have given them. Often on Raksha Bandhan, young men spend the day parading around in the streets, showing off their rakhi. It is a great honor to receive a rakhi, since it shows that someone cares greatly for you.

*Opposite:* This little girl is tying a rakhi on her baby brother. In return, he gives her some fruit and money.

# THINGS FOR YOU TO DO

If you were in India at festival time, you might want to play a game. How about Pachisi? *Pachisi* [pah-CHEE-see] has been played in India for hundreds of years. Indians still enjoy a good game of Pachisi today. It takes two, three, or four people. Each person will need some kind of playing piece, or token—either yellow, red, blue, or green. You will also need a die that is white on two sides and yellow, red, blue, and green on the other four sides. Use the playing board on the next page. The object is to move all the way around the board and then up the diagonal strip from your home square to the star in the center.

## How to play Pachisi

Put your marker in the corner of the board marked with your color. Have someone throw the die until a color comes up. The person with that color begins. Throw the die. If it comes up the same color as your marker, move one space counterclockwise and throw again. If it comes up white, don't move but throw again. If any other color comes up, your turn is over. The person on your right is next. Play continues in this way. The first person to get to the center wins.

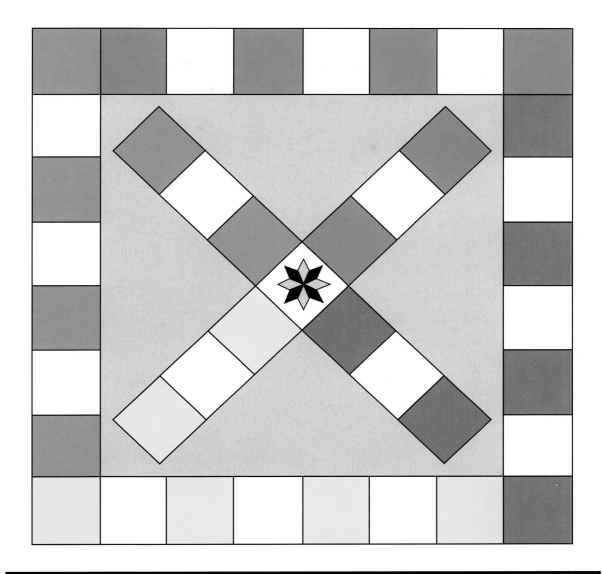

## Things to look for in your library

*The Elephant-Headed God and Other Hindu Tales*. Debjani Chatterjee (Oxford University Press Children's Books, 1993).

*Gandhi* (Columbia Pictures video, 1983).

*In Celebration*. Ravi Shankar (EMI CD, 1996).

*In the Village of the Elephants*. Jeremy Schmidt (Walker & Co., 1994).

*India: Country Topics for Crafts Projects*. Anita Ganeri and R. Wright (Franklin Watts, 1994).

*India: Games People Play*. Dale E. Howard (Children's Press, 1996).

*The Jungle Book*. Rudyard Kipling (Troll Classics, 1992).

*Making Music*. Zakir Hussain (ECM CD, 1994).

*Postcards from India*. Denise Allard (Raintree/Steck Vaughn, 1996).

*The Tiger and the Brahmin*. Ben Kingsley (Rabbit Ears Productions video, 1991).

# Make a Divali Lamp

Y ou can make your own Divali lamp to light your house at Divali. Use the kind of clay that hardens by itself unless you know someone with a kiln who can fire it for you. Real Divali lamps are filled with oil. Then a wick is put in and lit. We use a candle to be safer.

**You will need:**
1. Air-hardening clay
2. Tempera paint
3. Paintbrushes
4. Water
5. Candle

**1** Break off a handful of clay and roll it into a ball. Knead it well to make it soft enough to work with. Wet the clay from time to time as you work to keep it from drying out.

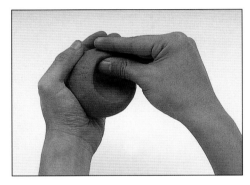

**2** Mold the clay into a lamp shape by hollowing out a well in the ball. Keep working the clay until the sides are the right thickness. Keep the clay thick around the edge to form a lip. Make the bottom flat so it will sit steady. When your lamp looks the way you want it, set it aside to dry.

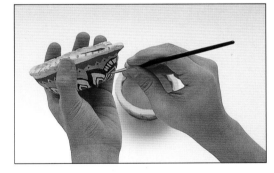

**3** When your lamp has dried all through, it's time to paint it. Use bright colors to make it look nice and bright. You can put some designs on the inside, too. After the paint has dried, put a candle inside and you're all done!

# MAKE BURFI

Here is a simple kind of Indian treat. Try making burfi for Divali. There are many different kinds of burfi made with different kinds of nuts and flours. After you've tried your own, look for a shop that sells Indian snacks and sample some other kinds. You're sure to like them!

**You will need:**
1. 1 pound (.5 kg) raw cashews
2. Blender
3. 1 cup (240 ml) sweetened condensed milk
4. Butter
5. Pastry brush
6. 1 teaspoon flour
7. Measuring spoons
8. Small saucepan
9. Frying pan
10. Baking tray
11. Wooden spoon
12. Knife

**1** Put the cashews in a frying pan and cook them over low heat, stirring constantly, until they are golden brown. Be careful not to burn them!

**2** Grind the roasted cashews. You can use a blender or crush them with a rolling pin.

**3** Mix half the ground cashews, the condensed milk, and the flour in a saucepan. Cook the mixture for a few minutes until it is almost solid.

**4** Grease the baking tray with the butter. Press the cashew mixture into the greased pan. Pour the remaining cashews over the top and press them into the mixture. Let it cool and then cut into squares.

# GLOSSARY

| | |
|---|---|
| *Baharat Nhatyam*, 11 | A traditional dance of India. |
| *bhangra*, 6 | A folkdance performed by Sikh men at Baisakhi. |
| **Caucasians**, 4 | White people who settled in India. |
| **Dravidians**, 4 | Dark-skinned people who lived in India long ago. |
| **Hindi**, 3 | The official language of northern India. |
| *Kathak*, 11 | A traditional Indian dance using bells around the ankles. |
| lunar, 6 | Following the phases of the moon. |
| *mahatma*, 10 | A title of respect meaning "Great Soul." |
| *mela*, 3 | A fair. |
| *rakhi*, 24 | A bracelet given to brothers on Raksha Bandhan. |
| **Rangoli designs**, 23 | Designs drawn on the doorstep with chalk or colored flour. |
| sitar, 11 | An Indian stringed instrument with a long neck. |
| tabla, 11 | A pair of drums of different sizes used in Indian music. |
| vegetarian, 23 | Someone who eats no meat or fish. |

# INDEX